No Road Back

Written by Rachel Russ

Illustrated by Alessandro D'urso

Collins

Cass is in the go-kart. With a sharp turn, she avoids a log.

But the go-kart hits a rock, tips, then turns.

Now it is dark. Cass sits in a car.

She sees the finish far down the road.

A map pops up: Get to the finish to go back.

I cannot fail, thinks Cass.

She sets off.

A red-hot ring pops up. Hot air fills the car.

Zoom! The car shoots up.

A gap!

Cass looks down.

The car thuds down.

The roots of an oak hit the road.

Cass avoids them with a quick turn.

"The finish!" Cass yells.

Finish

Now the car turns.

Map

Go-kart

Car

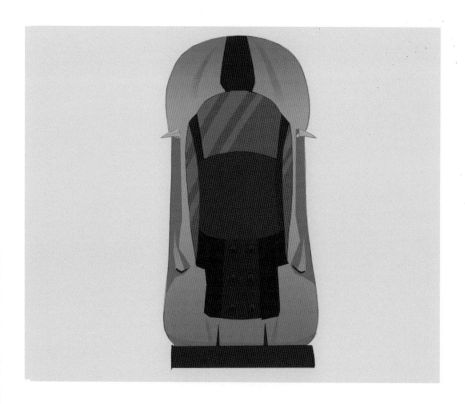

The road was hard.

But I had to get back.

Cass

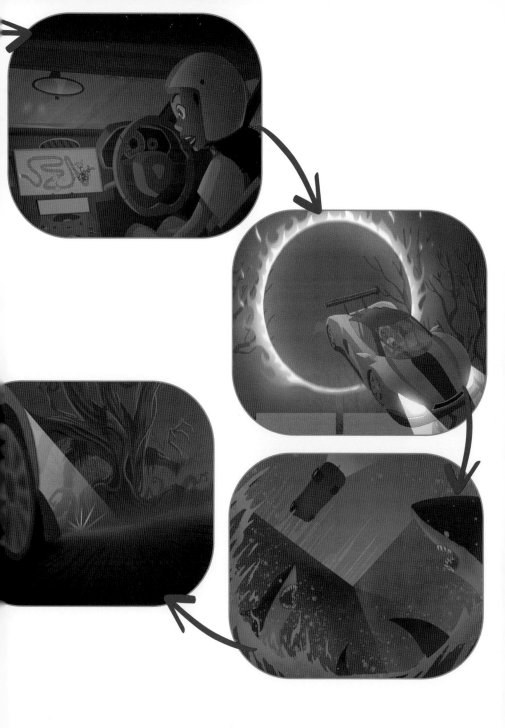

🐾 Review: After reading 🐾

Use your assessment from hearing the children read to choose any GPCs, words or tricky words that need additional practice.

Read 1: Decoding

- On page 7 point to the word **fail**. Ask: If Cass did fail, what do you think might have happened? Encourage the children to reread pages 6 and 7 before answering. (e.g. *she wouldn't have reached the finish*) Discuss other contexts in which people don't want to fail. (e.g. *in a television quiz*)
- On page 10, point to the "oo" in **zoom** and ask: What sound does this digraph make? (*long /oo/*) Repeat for "oo" in **looks** on page 11. (*short /oo/*) Encourage the children to sound out the words.
  o On page 12, repeat for: "oa" in **road**   "oi" in **avoids**   "ur" in **turn**
- Point to the speech bubble on page 15 and ask the children: Can you blend in your head as you read these words aloud?

Read 2: Prosody

- Challenge the children to read pages 10 and 11 using a storyteller voice to create atmosphere and excitement.
- Ask them to think about reading fast to show how the car is zooming along, and emphasis for when the car **thuds** down. Say: Don't forget to put feeling into Cass's voice when you read the speech bubble.
- Let the children take turns to read a page. Encourage positive feedback.

Read 3: Comprehension

- Ask the children if they have been in a go-kart or seen a car race. What was it like? What happened?
- Focus on pages 3 and 4, and discuss why the go-kart has changed into a car. (*Cass is imagining she is in a car race*)
- Turn to pages 22 and 23 and ask the children to retell the story from Cass's point of view. Ask questions such as: What are you thinking here? What happens to you? What's in the way? Children could mime sitting in the driving seat as they explain what's happening.
- Bonus content: Look together at pages 16 and 17. Encourage the children to predict other things that Cass might imagine along the track. Ask: What might happen if the car dropped into the tank? Is there a button she could push to lift up the car?
- Bonus content: Encourage the use of technical language to compare the go-kart and car on pages 18 and 19. For example: Which might go faster? Why? Are the wheels different? In what way?